T0095604

Growing
in
Grace

Growing in Grace

in

Grace

Etta Boone

authorHOUSE®

AuthorHouse™
1663 Liberty Drive
Bloomington, IN 47403
www.authorhouse.com
Phone: 1-800-839-8640

© 2012 by Etta Boone. All rights reserved.

All Scriptures are taken from the King James Version

No part of this book may be reproduced, stored in a retrieval system, or transmitted by any means without the written permission of the author.

Published by AuthorHouse   08/14/2012

ISBN: 978-1-4772-5704-3 (sc)
ISBN: 978-1-4772-5705-0 (e)

Any people depicted in stock imagery provided by Thinkstock are models, and such images are being used for illustrative purposes only. Certain stock imagery © Thinkstock.

This book is printed on acid-free paper.

Because of the dynamic nature of the Internet, any web addresses or links contained in this book may have changed since publication and may no longer be valid. The views expressed in this work are solely those of the author and do not necessarily reflect the views of the publisher, and the publisher hereby disclaims any responsibility for them.

Table of Contents

We all pass through the six biological stages of growing up namely (1) infant, (2) toddler, (3) adolescent, (4) teenager, (5) Adult and (6) senior citizen.

Infant—is the earliest stage. This is the baby stage. In other words a very young child.

Toddler—walking unsteadily, not sure yet inquisitive (prying)

Adolescent—youth the time of life between childhood and adulthood (the formative years)

Teenager—years of one's life from 13 through 19

Adult—grown up, mature (usually considered 20 and up)

Senior Citizen—usually 55 and older

 Dedication

Thanks to God and Archbishop Harris E. Clark for imparting in me to write this book; 2 Chronicles 20:20b:

> "Believe in the Lord your God, so shall you be established; Believe His prophets, so shall you prosper."

Thank you to my dear friend Barbara Davis and my computer instructor Apostle Terry Forbes; without whom this book would not be completed.

The purpose of this book is to help you know and understand our Heavenly Father. It is to help those

---

who feel like they are lost, don't fit in, confused or just struggling with being saved or the call on their life.

Grace has many definitions; the blessing of food is one, moving eloquently or gracefully is another; delay granted for payment due (grace period) is another definition of grace.

The grace that I am talking about is that undeserving favor that God bestows upon us. It is the love that He displays toward us even when we know that we are not in right standing with Him.

May you find guidance, peace and deliverance while you are reading this book; may you gain a closer walk with our Savior, Jesus Christ.

There are two stages in our life as we grow into maturity; naturally or spiritually.

Apostle Etta M. Boone

Infant and Toddler

An infant or new born baby already has a strong determination to have its own way. (I'll call it a controlling spirit) Because of the excitement, we think that our baby is the cutest thing and we are not aware of what's going on; for instance when babies want attention they will cry until they get what they want; hungry, soiled or just plain cranky they will cry until they get what they want. You might say that is just life. (Maybe) but after the baby has been bathed, fed, changed and played with there is no need to jump at every beckoning cry.

Parenting starts at the birth of the baby. This is when you begin training your baby with love and correction.

Proverbs Chapter 22:6 states:

"Train up a child in the way he should go;
and when he is old, he will not
depart from it."

(Be careful not to become abusive)

I was born in 1940 to an unwed mother, I never knew my father. From infant to the age of six, I was raised by my mother's aunt who was a God fearing woman. She taught me my first prayer:

"Now I lay me down to sleep, I pray the Lord my soul to keep, if I should die before I wake I pray the Lord my soul to take."

This is a very powerful prayer that I recited faithfully without understanding the meaning. By teaching me the importance of prayer, my aunt was indirectly making me realize that I needed to have God in my life. I learned that it is possible to pray to God without knowing who He is.

Adolescent

My mother married my stepfather when I was six years old. They brought me to live with them in the city of Baltimore, Maryland. This was a new experience for me. I had never seen row houses before or houses without porches; I never seen street cars before nor did I know what segregation was all about.

At first things were all right in our house. But later things were different because there was no prayer and there was much drinking and fighting between my parents. Two years later my aunt that raised me died in North Carolina and I could not go to the funeral because there was no money. Then my world was turned upside down;

my stepfather began molesting me sexually. He put fear in me and expressly declared that I dare not tell my mother or anyone. I was scared and hurting. School gave me the opportunity to escape the torture; but only for a few hours of the day. I applied myself to my school work because of the relief that school offered me.

I was the only child at that time. My oldest brother was born nine years later followed by six more children; four brothers and two sisters. My siblings were treated a little better than me but not much. I became angry, hateful and down-right mean. I had to look out for my siblings as well as my mother because of the abuse by my stepfather. My baby sister would help me with the younger boys because of my stepfather being so mean.

My stepfather's sexual molestation took me to another level of anger. I was in a situation where I couldn't tell my mother or anyone else. (If you are being molested tell someone) I couldn't tell my mother because she couldn't help herself; my stepfather would buy whiskey and make her drink until she was drunk. That's when the molestation would begin. When this moment came, My aunt's prayer would come to my mind.

"Now I lay me down to sleep, I pray the Lord my soul to keep, if I should die before I wake I pray the Lord my soul to take"

Being much older now, I promised my stepfather; that if he touched me one more time, I would **kill** him. (Harboring hatred or anger in one's mind will lead to all kinds of evil thoughts; and later those thoughts will be put into action.

Teenager

The teenage years are very important to you; this is the age from 13 to 19. It is a time when you should be focusing on your future; you have 6 years to mold the rest of your life. The Jewish custom has a religious ceremony for boys at the age of 13 and girls at the age of 12 that is called a Bar Mitzvah or Bat Mitzvah; at this time they are responsible for following Jewish law.

They are morally responsible for their own actions; the young males are eligible to be called to read the Torah or participate in a Minyan. The young women experience some form of discrimination in the Orthodox Jewish ceremonies because they are not allowed to participate in the reading of the Torah.

In your young lives you may experience many adversities that seem unfair or cruel; but through them all if you learn to trust God and get to know Him life can be much better for you.

A recent study taken in March 2008 showed that 1 out of 4 teenage girls were infected with sexual transmitted diseases (STD). Not only are they having unprotected sex, but are at risk to contract HIV or AIDS. HIV and AIDS are deadly diseases with no known cure at this time. They are diseases that can be passed on to an unborn baby.

We are living in a day when teenagers are killing their whole families; they are becoming drug addicts and are living hopeless lives. The majority of their parents are in prison or they are living in a one parent home usually the mother who has to work. The internet is now the baby sitter where there is much immorality and danger. Don't become prey to these dangers. Take charge of your life; make Jesus your Lord and Savior, read your Bible and live a victorious life.

 Adult

I became pregnant at the age of eighteen and later I got married. This was a mistake because I was seeking love and comfort at the wrong time and for the wrong reason. Fornication should not be part of an unwed individual's life. 1 Corinthians 6:18:

> "Flee fornication. Every sin that a man doeth is without the body: but he that committeth fornication sinneth against his own body".

Now I am adult, married at the age of 18, separated at age 27 with three little children; no peace or contentment. I went on welfare for about two months, it was not enough money for me and my children (thank God) I went to work. There was no support money from my husband because he would quit his job to keep from paying child support. Now let me make this clear; all the trouble that I was having in my marriage was not all my husband's fault. First, I did not know how to be neither a wife nor he a husband.

My marriage was not a happy one; I loved my husband but I married for the wrong reason. I was trying to run from all of the hurt that I had known in my life. I did not have a positive example as to what a happy marriage should be like. There was no positive role model for me to follow; so I took what I had seen and heard from what I had to live within my youth. I also took another promise with me and that was no man would hit or mistreat me. (I'll call this *baggage*—things that are in our past that we have not dealt with or been delivered from.)

My husband told me after we had three children that my mother had begged him to marry me.

That was a shock to me; we had been fighting and arguing all this time and he tells me this. I laid him and my mother out and made plans for my life with my children and without my husband. ("Now I lay me down to sleep, I pray the Lord my soul to keep, if I should die before I wake, I pray the Lord my soul to take.")

I had no idea what the Bible said about marriage. This is a mistake that is made today with people that are planning marriage. They base what Hollywood and today's society is doing to be the mind set for their marriage. They go into marriage with their solution all ready. I'll get a divorce.

This is definitely wrong according to the Word of God. Divorce will put you in an adulterous situation with God. There are many in the body of Christ that does not agree with the Word of God; when it comes to marriage.

I had male friends, but I preferred married men because there was no strings attached; and because

I didn't know the value of marriage or how to be married and I had a lot of *baggage* in my life. There was nothing to compare my marriage to. If you are in this situation with this mind set; stop, read, and listen to the Word of God. (Ephesians 5: 22-25 "Wives, submit yourselves unto your own husbands, as unto the Lord. For the husband is the head of the wife, even as Christ is the head of the church: and He is the savior of the body.)

Therefore as the church is subject unto Christ, so let the wives be to their own husbands in everything. Husbands, love your wives even as Christ also loved the church and gave himself for it." Colossians 3:18-19 "Wives, subject yourselves unto your own husbands, as it is fit in the Lord. Husbands, love your wives, and be not bitter against them." We are emotional beings that usually determine the answer to a situation by the way we feel; when we should be basing over situations upon the word of God. Proverbs 3:5-6 "Trust in the Lord with all thine heart: and lean not unto your own understanding. In all thy ways acknowledge him, and He shall direct thy paths."

Marriage was instituted in the beginning by God. It was a union between a man and a woman. (Adam and Eve—Genesis 2:21-24; "And the Lord God caused a deep sleep to fall upon Adam, and he slept: and God took one of his(Adam) ribs, and closed up the flesh instead thereof, and the rib, which the Lord God had taken from man, made He a woman, and brought her unto the man. And Adam said this is now bone of my bones, and flesh of my flesh: she shall be called Woman, because she was taken out of Man. Therefore shall a man leave his father and mother, and shall cleave unto his wife: and they shall be one flesh."

Marriage should not be taken lightly; there should be no outside interference in a marriage it is a life time commitment according to the Word of God.—Matthew19:3-9 "The Pharisees also came unto Him (Jesus), tempting Him, and saying unto Him, is it lawful for a man to put away his wife for every cause? And He (Jesus) answered and said unto them. Have you not read that He (God) who made them at the beginning made them male and female? And said, for this cause shall a man leave Father and Mother, and shall cleave to his wife: and they twain shall be one flesh? Wherefore they are no more twain, but one flesh. What therefore God hath joined together, let not man put asunder. They say unto Him, why did Moses then command to give a writing of divorcement, and to put her away? He (Jesus) saith to them, Moses because of the hardness of your hearts suffered you to put away your wives: but from the beginning it was not so. And I (Jesus) say unto you, whosoever shall put away his wife, except it be for fornication, and shall marry another, committeth adultery: and whoso marrieth her who is put away doth commit adultery. Jesus the Savior is speaking.

1Corinthians 7: 10-11 "And to the married I (Paul) command, yet not I, but the Lord (Jesus) let not the wife depart from her husband: but and if she depart, let her remain unmarried, or be reconciled to her husband: and let not the husband put away his wife.

Marriage is being redefined by society to be between male and male or woman and woman, which *is* definitely against the Word of God.

Our society has redefined marriage; it is no longer a union between a man and woman. Laws are in place in some states to legalize marriage to be a union between same sex couples. This is totally against the Word of God. Genesis 2:21-25—And the Lord God caused a deep sleep to fall upon Adam, and he slept: and He took one of his ribs, and closed up the flesh instead thereof. And the rib, which the Lord God had taken from man, made he a woman and brought her unto the man. And Adam said, this is now bone of my bones, and flesh of my flesh; and she shall be called Woman because she was taken out of Man. Therefore shall a man leave his father and his mother, and shall cleave unto his wife; and they shall be one flesh.)

The foundation for marriage was started in the Garden of Eden; by God.

If you are considering marriage; get to know your mate, not sexually but his or her ways. See how they treat their parents; find out what their goals are in life. Make sure that they are not controlling or unstable about things of life and most of all do they believe in your God. What is their belief? (2 Corinthians 6:14—Be ye not unequally yoked together with unbelievers; for what fellowship hath righteousness? And what communion hath light with darkness?)

Women you must submit to your husband; this is something that I wasn't going to do. Remember that I had made a promise that no man was going to mistreat me; so I had to be in control. This is why you must be delivered from past hurts. (Ephesians 5:22-26-Wives, submit yourselves unto your own husbands, as unto the Lord. For the husband is the head of the wife, even as Christ is the head of the church: and He is the savior of the body. Therefore as the church is subject unto Christ, so let the wives be to their own husbands in everything. Husbands, love your wives, even as Christ also loved the church, and gave himself for it; that He might sanctify and cleanse it with the washing of water by the word.) (Colossians 3:18-21-Wives, submit yourselves unto your own husbands, as it is fit in the Lord. Husbands, love your wives, and be not bitter against them. Children, obey your parents in all things for this is well pleasing unto the Lord.) Not being saved I had no clue about the Word of God. Read your Word daily; and get to know your Savior; His plan for your life.

If you are used to having your own way; then you are a selfish person that need to change your attitude; you will be the controlling force in the marriage. It matters not if you are male or female. If you are female you will not submit unto your mate; if you are a male you will be controlling. Marriage is an equal opportunity union. (1 Corinthians 7: 2-4-Nevertheless, to avoid fornication, let every man have his own wife, and let every woman have her own husband. Let the husband render unto the wife due benevolence: and likewise also the wife unto the husband. The wife hath not power of her own body, but the husband and likewise also the husband hath not power of his own body, but the wife) Remember that God ordained marriage and He knew what He wanted; Do it His way and be happy during your struggles. (There will be struggles, ups and downs; but through it all you will make it; if you do it God's way.)

The New Birth

I accepted Jesus as my personal Savior on October 4, 1981 at the age of forty one. Forty one years that had many ups and downs, Years that I was growing in the Grace of God and did not know it; so many times we do not recognize that some one behind the scene is watching and helping us. That someone is Jesus—Hallelujah.

Things in my life were a lot clearer because I began to read the Word of God. I began to realize that everything that I had experienced in the past that God was already there. When I thought that I couldn't make it, I made it. (Now I lay me down to sleep, I pray the Lord my soul to keep, if I should die before I wake, I pray the Lord my soul to take.) Let's talk about prayer; it's not how long or short your prayer might be, but the sincerity of the prayer.

Prayer is a powerful tool that God has given to the believers; it is a way that we communicate with Him. Prayer is a God given right. John 14: 13-14 "And whatsoever ye shall ask in my name, that will I do, that the Father may be glorified in the Son. If you shall ask anything in my name, I will do it. Read the Bible so that you would know the will of God for your life and take advantage of it. Talk to Him when you can't talk to anyone else; He always have a listening ear.

Romans 8: 26-27 "Likewise the Spirit also helpeth our infirmities: for we know not what we should pray for as we ought: but the Spirit itself maketh intercession for us with groaning which cannot be uttered. And He that searcheth the hearts knoweth what is the mind of the Spirit, because He maketh intercession for the saints according to the will of God."

John 14: 26 "But the Comforter, which is the Holy ghost, whom the Father will send in my name, (Jesus) He shall teach you all things, and bring all things to your remembrance, whatsoever I have said unto you" It is very important that you have a relationship with the Lord in order to receive the gift of the Holy Ghost.

As a baby Christian, I was excited and happy and was receiving everything that I ask for. I was getting what I wanted when I wanted it, I was spoiled. I call my adolescence and teenager years as a Christians as my on the job training years. I was called into the ministry at the age of forty-five, four years after being saved. Much like today women were not really accepted in ministry. So here I am not delivered, feeling insecure and definitely not qualified with a call on my life; I began the walk that led me where I am today.

Romans 8: 28 "And we know that all things work together for good to them that love God, to them who are the called according to His purpose." God has a purpose for your life no matter what your background may be. Stay encouraged you are still growing in grace.

If you are a babe in Christ, you must submit to someone in authority. Hebrews 13: 17 "Obey them that have the rule over you, and submit yourselves: for they watch for your souls, as they that must give account, that they may do it with joy, and not with grief: for that is unprofitable for you.

It is very important that you have a Spiritual Father or Mother figure in your life. There is a need for guidance in your life spiritually as well as naturally. You can save yourself a lot of headaches by seeking wise counsel. Proverbs 11:14 "Where no counsel is, the people fall: but in the multitude of counselors there is safety" Just like you had to submit to your parents; you must be accountable to someone in the ministry.

We are living in a day where the Word of God is being changed everyday according to how we feel; instead of what the Word says. So get some instruction from someone that is seasoned in the Word of God; and are living the life of a Christian. Remember you are still Growing in Grace and there is a lot to be learned. Do not depend solely on the advice of others, when you are seeking counseling; keep God first. You must know the voice of God. It is very important that you be filled with the Holy Ghost; He will be your helper. (John 14: 26-But the Comforter, which is the Holy Ghost, whom the Father will send in my name, He shall teach you all things, and bring all things to you remembrance, whatsoever I have said unto you.)

Those of you that are called; don't get to the place that you know it all. Mistakes will be made, feelings will be hurt, your gift will be ignored; just remember who called you and trust that He knows what He is doing. Proverbs 18: 16 "A man's gift maketh room for him, and bringeth him before great men" Don't try to open doors on your own; God will do this for you.

Remember our goal in life should be to live; so that we will reign forever with our Lord and Savior Jesus Christ. All ways keep God and His Word first in your life; and make all of your decisions according to the Word of God. And remember that there are consequences to your decisions that will affect not only you; but everyone that is connected to you.

Jesus said in Matthew 11:28-30 "Come unto Me all ye that labor and are heavy laden and I will give you rest. Take My yoke upon you, and learn of me; for I am meek and lowly in heart; and ye shall find rest for your souls. For My yoke is easy and My burden is light."

Don't take the Word of God lightly; hold it dear to your heart. You will find that it is the most important thing in your life. You will find peace, happiness, joy, instructions and so many enjoyable things in the Word of God. Put God first in everything that you do. Get to know His voice; and that will be by His Word.

Adult and Senior

I am seventy years old now and I am still Growing in Grace. I have faced betrayals, many heartaches and the loss of so called friends; yet I wouldn't change any part of my life. Your past with all of the ups and downs and all of the disappointments that came your way; will help you to know the power of prayer and most of all the love of our Heavenly Father. I am praying the Word of God and walking in the promises of God.

God has used me to win many souls to Him. I did prison ministry for many years; and I have a church with member that have been delivered from drugs, and released from prison and come from all walks of life. We all are still growing in grace.

You that are struggling with your faith or the call on your life; don't lean to your own understanding; don't try to figure things out, just Grow in the Grace of God. He'll never leave or forsake you (Matthew 28: 18-20-And Jesus came and spoke unto them, saying, all power is given unto me in heaven and in earth. Go ye therefore, and teach all nations, baptizing them in the name of the Father, and of the Son, and of the Holy Ghost. Teaching them to observe all things whatsoever I have commanded you: and lo, I am with you always, even unto the end of the world. Amen) be willing to confess your faults. (James 5:16,—Confess your fault one to another, and pray one for another, that ye may be healed. The effectual fervent prayer of a righteous man availeth much.) (Revelation12:11-And they overcame him by the blood of the Lamb and by the word of their testimony, and they loved not their lives unto the death.) When we talk about our problems, we expose Satan and he can't get a strong hold on you.

The New Birth

Man was created in the image and likeness of God and was given a will. (Power of choice) (Genesis 1:27-28 So God created man in his own image, in the image of God created he him; male and female created he them. And God blessed them, and God said unto them, be fruitful, and multiply, and replenish the earth, and subdue it: and have dominion over the fish of the sea, and over the fowl of the air, and over every living thing that moveth upon the earth.) They were blessed; all they had to do was be obedient to God; same as today all we have to do is to be obedient to the Word of God.

It was the will of man that got him in trouble with God. The will of man is connected with the flesh of man; therefore making him carnal (worldly) minded which enmity (ill will) against God is. (Romans 8:5-6—For they that are after the flesh do mind the things of the flesh; but they that are after the Spirit the things of the spirit. For to be carnally minded is death; but to be spiritually minded is life and peace.) there is a need for someone (Jesus) to turn us back to the obedience of God.

The born again experience (John 3:3—Jesus answered and said unto him, verily, verily, I say unto you, except a man be born again, he cannot see the kingdom of God.) This takes place when we accept Jesus as our personal Savior. (Romans 10: 9-10—That if you confess with your mouth the Lord Jesus, and shall believe in your heart that God has raised Him from the dead, you shall be saved. For with the heart man believes unto righteousness: and with the mouth confession is made unto salvation.)

We must be willing to surrender our will to God's will according to the Word of God. Now back on the road that will lead us back to the Tree of Life; Paul lets us know that we must change the way we think and act. (Romans 12:2—And be not conformed to this world: but be transformed by the renewing of your mind, that you may prove what is that good, and acceptable, and perfect will of God.) You will make mistakes; but remember that the Holy Spirit is there to help you. (John 14: 16 & 26—and I will pray the father, and He shall give you another Comforter, that He may abide with you forever. But the Comforter, which the Holy Ghost, whom the Father will send in My name. He shall teach you all things, and bring to your remembrance, whatever I have said unto you.)

When man disobeyed God in the beginning; when He told them not to touch or eat from the tree in the midst of the garden that they would die He meant a spiritual death. Up into the disobedience of Adam and Eve the Spirit of God was the controlling force of man; after the fall of Man satan was the controlling force. (John 12: 31—Now is the judgment of this world, now shall the prince (satan) of this world be cast out.) (2 Corinthians 4:4—In whom the god of this world has blinded the minds of them which believe not, lest the light of the glorious gospel of Christ, who is the image of God, should shine unto them)

Satan is a defeated for (Matthew 28:18—And Jesus came and spoke to them, saying all power is given unto Me in heaven and in earth.) and (1 John 3:8b—For this purpose the Son of God was manifested, that He might destroy the works of the devil.) Jesus is Lord of Lords and King of Kings and since He is our Savior we have the same power over Satan. Hallelujah! If you haven't given your life to Christ yet; do it now!

Epilogue

I am a divorced woman of God that is living according to the Word of God; (1 Corinthians 7: 10-11—And unto the married, I command, yet not I, but the Lord. Let not the wife depart from her husband; but and if she depart, let her remain unmarried, or be reconciled to her husband; and let not the husband put away his wife.) I did not get peace with this until I yielded myself to the Word of God. I couldn't listen to other people nor let my flesh rule my decision. It was not easy; but God is true to His Word; He'll give you peace in the midst of a storm. Hallelujah! Don't forget that the flesh will not agree with the word of God, so you must rely on the word of God. The word of God increases your faith (Romans 10:17-So then faith cometh by hearing, and hearing by the word of God.)

Remember the promise of our Savior that He would be with us always.

May the words of this book bless you and help you with your walk with Jesus the Savior of the world as you Grow in Grace.

Love always,
Apostle Etta M. Boone